5TH COUNCIL OF CARTHAGE

Synod of the African Church 397 AD

St. Aurelius
Archbishop of Carthage

Translated by: D.P. Curtin

5TH COUNCIL OF CARTHAGE

Copyright @ 2010 Dalcassian Press

All rights reserved. No part of this publication may be reproduced, distributed, or transmitted in any form or by any means, including photocopying, recording, or other electronic or mechanical methods, without the prior written permission of the publisher, except in the case of brief quotations embodied in critical reviews and certain other non-commercial uses permitted by copyright law. For permission request, write to Dalcassian Press at dalcassianpublishing at gmail.com

ISBN: 979-8-8693-9662-4 (Paperback)

Library of Congress Control Number:
Author: Curtin, D.P. (1985-)

Printed by Ingram Content Group, 1 Ingram Blvd, La Vergne, Tennessee

First printing edition 2010.

THE THIRD COUNCIL OF CARTHAGE

HELD BY THE FORTY-SEVEN BISHOPS, IN THE ERA 436, TO CAESAR AND ATTICUS, THE MOST ILLUSTRIOUS COUNCULS

5TH OF SEPTEMBER, [397 AD]

At Carthage, in the secretary of the restored basilica, when the bishop Aurelius had taken his seat together with his co-bishops, the deacons also being present, these things were established which were defined in the present council.

I. That the provincial bishops should inquire about their primacy at Easter.

It was therefore decided at first, because of the error which often occurs, that all the bishops of the African provinces should take care to accept the observance of the Easter day from the Church of Carthage.

II. That a council be held every year.

In the same way, it was decided that for ecclesiastical causes, which often grow old to the destruction of the people, a council should be called every year, to which all the provinces which have the first seats should send two or as many bishops as legates from their councils; that there may be less unpopular and less expensive guests, and that in the assembled assembly there may be full authority: but from Tripoli, on account of the scarcity of bishops, let one bishop come.

III. That the bishop should acknowledge the canons before he is ordained.

Likewise, it was decided that, when ordaining bishops or clerics, the decrees of the councils should first be impressed upon their ears by their ordinators, so that they would not repent of having done anything contrary to the statutes of the council.

IV. That the young and virgins should not be married before the age of twenty-five years.

Also, it was decided that before twenty-five years of age neither deacons should be ordained, nor virgins ordained, and that readers should not greet the people.

V. That the sacrament of catechumens should not be given.

Likewise, it was decided that even during the most solemn Easter days the sacrament of catechumens should not be given, except with the usual salt. because if the faithful do not change the sacraments during those days, neither should the catechumens change.

VI. That baptism or the eucharist is not given to the dead.

Also, it was decided that the Eucharist should not be given to the bodies of the dead; for it was said by the Lord: Receive and eat: but corpses can neither receive nor eat. Then we must be careful lest the weakness of the brethren believe that even the dead can be baptized, to whom they have not noticed that the Eucharist is given.

VII. As if a bishop is accused, where or below what time he is examined.

Aurelius the bishop said: Whoever is accused of the bishops, the accuser must bring the case to the primates of his province, and he must not be suspended from communion to whom the crime is intended, unless he is summoned to state his case by letter from the first see at least on the appointed day, that is within the space of a month from the day on which he received the letter He agreed: that if he proved any real causes of necessity, which it was obvious that he could not meet, he would have full opportunity to state his reasons within another month; however, long after the second month, he will not communicate until he is cleansed. If, however, he does not wish to meet at the annual universal council, so that his cause may be ended there, he is judged to have pronounced the sentence of damnation in himself; at the time when he does not communicate, nor does he communicate in his church or parish: but his accuser, if he is never absent during the days of the cause to be told, shall not be removed from communion; but if at any time he was absent withdrawing himself, the bishop being restored to communion, the accuser himself shall be removed from communion, yet in such a way that he himself is not deprived of the opportunity of carrying out the cause, if he has proved that he was not willing to meet for the day, but was unable. It was decided, however, that when he began to act in the judgment of the bishops, if the person of the accuser was guilty, he should not be admitted to plead, unless he wished to plead his own causes, and not, however, if he wished to assert ecclesiastical ones.

VIII. Concerning priests and deacons, how many bishops should hear them.

But if priests or deacons have been accused, the bishop appointed to him from the neighboring places with a legitimate number of colleagues, together with him in the name of the bishop six in the name of the bishop, three in the name of the deacon, let them discuss their case, with the same days and delay and from the communion of removals and discussion of persons between the accusers and them those who are charged with the preserved form. As for the cases of the rest of the clerics, the local bishop alone recognizes and decides.

IX. That the clerics should not appeal to the public courts.

Likewise, it was decided that any of the bishops, priests and deacons or clerics, when a crime has been instituted against him in the Church or a civil case has been moved, if he has left the ecclesiastical judgment and wants to be cleansed by the public judgments, even if a sentence has been pronounced for him, he shall lose his place; and this in a criminal action: but in a civil action he must lose what he has driven out, if he prefers to take his place. For he who has the authority to elect judges from all parts of the Church, judges himself unworthy of the Church's association, who, feeling bad about the whole Church, asks for the help of a secular judgement, when the Apostle commands that the cases of private Christians should also be brought to the Church and determined there.

X. If each one has been from other ecclesiastical judges to others, do not obey the former if a different opinion is given.

This was also decided, so that any ecclesiastical judges who have been challenged by other ecclesiastical judges, where there is greater authority, do not stand against those whose sentence has been resolved, if they could not be convinced that they had judged either with an enemy's heart, or had been corrupted by some greed or favor; have been, it is not permitted to be provoked even by a smaller number than was established.

XI. That the children of the clergy should not go to the spectacles.

That the sons of priests or clerics should not present secular spectacles, but neither should they watch them, since even all the laity are prohibited from watching them; for this has always been forbidden to all Christians, so that they do not approach where there is blasphemy.

XII. That the children of clerics should not be associated with the marriages of unbelievers.

It was also decided that the sons or daughters of bishops or any clerics should not be married to Gentiles or heretics or schismatics.

XIII. That the clerics should convey nothing of their affairs to unbelievers.

That bishops or clerics should contribute nothing to those who are not Catholic Christians, even if they were blood relatives, by donations of their property.

XIV. That clerics should not allow their children to go out of their power, unless they were proved by age and character.

That bishops or clerics should not allow their children to go out of their power by emancipation, unless they were sure of their deaths and of their age, so that their sins could already belong to them.

XV. That clerics should not be employers or businessmen.

Likewise, it was decided that bishops, priests and deacons, or clerics, should not be employers or agents of private individuals, nor should they seek a living by any base or dishonorable business, because they must look to what is written: No one serving God involves himself in worldly affairs.

XVI. That no clerk should be a usurer.

That no one of the clerics should receive more than what he has arranged for him: if money, let him receive money; if specie, specie: let him receive as much as he has given: and whatever else, only as much as he has given.

XVII. That foreign women should not cohabit with clerics.

That foreign women should not cohabit with all clerics, but only mothers, grandmothers, and aunts, aunts, sisters, and daughters of brothers or sisters, and whatever of the domestic family of necessity, even before they were ordained, already lived with them, or if their children had already been ordained with their parents. they took wives, or having no servants at home to marry, it was necessary to marry from elsewhere.

XVIII. That clerics may not be ordained unless all those who are with them are faithful.

That bishops and priests and deacons should not be ordained until all who are in their house have become Catholic Christians.

XIX. That clerics, when they have come to puberty, must either profess marriage or chastity.

It was decided that the readers, when they reached the age of puberty, were forced either to marry wives or to profess continence.

XX. That another bishop may not usurp foreign peoples.

It was agreed that foreign peoples should not be usurped by any bishop, nor should any of the bishops exceed the diocese of his colleague.

XXI. That no bishop dare retain or ordain a foreign cleric.

So that no one dares to retain or promote a foreign cleric, unless with the consent of his bishop, in the church entrusted to him: but the name of clerics is also retained by the readers and psalmists and porters.

XXII. That no clergyman should be ordained, unless he was of probable life.

That no cleric should be ordained unless approved either by the examination of the bishops or by the testimony of the people.

XXIII. Of prayers.

So that no one in prayers names either the Father for the Son, or the Son for the Father; and when the altar is attended, the prayer is always addressed to the Father; and whoever describes the prayers to himself from elsewhere, should not use them unless he has first communicated them with instructions to the brethren.

XXIV. That the bread and the cup should be offered in the sacrifice.

That in the sacraments of the Lord's body and blood nothing more should be offered than the Lord himself delivered, that is, bread and wine mixed with water, and no more should be offered in the first fruits than of grapes and grain.

XXV. Let not the clergy or the rulers have access to virgins or widows alone.

That clerics or governors should not approach widows or virgins except by order or permission of bishops or priests, and that they should not do this alone, but with fellow clerics or with those with whom the bishop or priest has commanded; nor should the bishops or priests alone have access to such women, but where either the clergy are present or some serious Christians.

XXVI. As the bishop of the first see is not called the high priest.

So that the bishop of the first see is not called chief priest or high priest or anything of the sort, but only the bishop of the first see.

XXVII. That the clerks should not enter the shops.

That clerics should not enter shops for eating or drinking, except for the necessity of traveling.

XXVIII. That the bishop should not go further without the formation of the metropolitan.

That the bishops should not go beyond the sea, except with the advice of the bishop of the first see of each of their provinces, so that he may especially take form or recommendation from him.

XXIX. That the mass should be celebrated by the vows.

That the sacraments of the altar should be celebrated only by fasting men; for if commendation is to be made in the afternoon of some deceased, whether bishops or others, it should be done with prayers alone, if those who do it are found to have already dined.

XXX. So that no one should get together in the church.

That no bishops or clerics should congregate in the church, unless by chance passers-by need refreshment there: the people also should be prevented as far as possible from this kind of conviviality.

XXXI. That a mode of penitence may be given to those who repent according to their sin.

That the times of penitence may be decided upon by the discretion of the bishop according to the difference of their sins.

XXXII. That a priest may not reconcile a penitent except by order or in the absence of the bishop.

That a priest may not reconcile a penitent to an unconsulting bishop, unless the absence of the bishop is compelled by necessity: but any penitent is a public and most common crime, which shakes the whole Church; hands were laid upon him before the apse.

XXXIII. On the custody of sacred virgins.

So that sacred virgins, if they have been deprived of their parents by whom they were kept, the providence of the bishop, or the presbyter where the bishop is absent, are recommended to the monastery of virgins or to more serious women, so that those living together may guard one another, lest by wandering here and there they injure the opinion of the Church.

XXXIV. About baptizing the sick who can no longer speak.

As the sick, if they cannot answer for themselves, when they have given their testimony of their will, they are baptized.

XXXV. Reconciliation is not denied to apostates and stage-turned converts.

Grace or reconciliation is not denied to actors and actors and other such persons, or to apostates converted or returned to God.

XXXVI. So that the priest does not finish the chrism.

That a priest should not confide virgins without consulting the bishop; but the chrism will never be finished.

XXXVII. That clerics should not dwell unnecessarily in a foreign state.

That clerics should not remain in a foreign state, unless the local bishop or local presbyters see to their just causes.

XXXVIII. That it may not be permitted to transfer bishops.

And we suggest to us that commandment, which also seems to have been established in the plenary synod of Capuenza, that no rebaptisms, reorganizations, or transfers of bishops may be allowed to take place: for Crisconius, the bishop of Villaregi, abandoned by his people, invaded the church of Tubunia, and each of them was warned this day to leave it according to what had been established. He despised the people whom he had invaded. Against this we have indeed heard what had been pronounced confirmed; but we ask, according to what we have been commanded, that we should not disdain to give confidence: since by necessity itself, we should be free to go against the governor of the province according to the statutes of the most glorious princes, so that he who would not yield to the gentle admonition of the sanctity of the glass and amend the unlawful, may be immediately excluded by judicial authority. Bishop Aurelius said: The preserved form of discipline will not be appreciated if the appetite declines to withdraw modestly from your charity of the assembly, since it has been contemptuous and defiant, even making the assembly with judicial authority. Honoratus and Urbanus said to the bishops: Is this then pleasing to all? It was said by all the bishops: It is just, please.

XXXIX. That two bishops should not presume to ordain the pontiff.

The bishops Honoratus and Urbanus said: And this is a commandment to us, that since two bishops of Numidia, our nearest brothers, have presumed to ordain the pontiff, the ordinations of the bishops should not be celebrated except by twelve. Bishop Aurelius said: The ancient form will be preserved, so that no less than three, who have been ordained by the metropolitan, are sufficient to ordain a bishop; on account of the fact that perhaps in Tripoli and in Arzuge barbarian nations appear to be interposed; for even in Tripoli, as it is asserted, there are only five bishops, and perhaps one or two of the same number may be occupied by some necessity, for it is difficult for all to be able to meet with regard to any number. For even in this Church, to which your Holiness has been deigned to assemble, we have to ordain frequently and almost throughout the Sunday: shall I frequently be able to summon twelve or ten, or not much less, bishops? but it is easy for me to add two neighbors to my smallness: therefore your charity sees with me that this very thing cannot be observed.

XL. So that, while the bishop is being elected, if he has opponents, five priests must meet.

And this is to be decided, that when we meet to elect a bishop, if any contradiction should arise, because such things have happened with us, they should not presume to purify him who is to be ordained, but three should be required for the number of the aforesaid two or three, and in the same people to whom it is to be ordered that first the persons who contradict should be discussed, and lastly those that are objected should also be discussed; and when he has been cleansed before the public eye, he shall be ordered in this way at last. If this agrees with the mind of your holiness, let it be strengthened by the answer of your condescension. It was said by all the bishops: It is quite pleasing.

XLI. That every year the bishops coming to the council are also informed of the paschal solemnity by their primate.

The bishops Honoratus and Urbanus said: Since certain treaties are known about the council, we also add that we are commanded about the day of Easter, that we should always be instructed about the Church of Carthage, as has been said, and not under a narrow period of time. Bishop Aurelius said: If it seems to your sanctity, since we already mentioned above that we promised to meet each year to negotiate, and when we meet together, then the holy day of Easter will be published by the ambassadors who were present at the council. The bishops Honoratus and Urbanus said: Now we ask of the present assembly that you deign to inform our province about this day by letter. Bishop Aurelius said: It must be so.

XLII. That the populace, which has always been subject to the diocese, should not receive another bishop.

Epigonius the bishop said: This has been established by the priestly assembly in many councils, so that the plebs who are held in dioceses by bishops, which have never had bishops, may not except with the will of the bishop from whom they are held receive their own rulers, that is, bishops; when they receive something, they abhor the communion of the brethren, or at least when they have been corrupted, as if they claim dominion for themselves in a certain tyrannical citadel, because most of the priests, puffed up and stupid, raise their necks against the bishops, either by winning over the people to themselves with banquets, or at least by persuading them by evil, that they may want the same for themselves by illicit favor to appoint rectors, which indeed we hold to be a remarkable wish of your mind, religious brother Aurelius, because you have often oppressed them not by caring for such petitioners, but because of their evil thoughts and wrongly arranged councils I say this: It is not necessary to receive a rector that people who have always been subject to the diocese, and never he had his own bishop; therefore, if it pleases the whole most holy assembly, let what I have pursued be confirmed. Bishop Aurelius said: Our brothers and fellow priests, I do not resist the persecution, but I confess that I have done this and will do it.

XLIII. So that those who, despised by their people, refuse to come to the council and lose the people and their honor.

Of course, those who have been in agreement not only with regard to the Carthaginian Church, but with regard to the entire priestly association, for most of them are conspiring with their own people whom they deceive, as has been said, scratching their ears, flattering to seduce, men of a vicious life, or at least inflated and by this a confederacy of separatists, who think that their own people are incubating, and sometimes the defendants refuse to come to the council, fearing that their atrocities might be betrayed; I say, if it pleases me, that in this respect not only the dioceses should not be preserved, but also that their own Church, which is in bad favor with them, should be recognized in every way, so that they may be rejected by the public authority, and be removed from the principal chairs themselves: for it is necessary that he who clings to all the brethren and to the whole council that he should possess not only his own right, but also the dioceses; but in truth those who think themselves sufficient for their own people, despised by fraternal love, not only lose their dioceses, but, as I have said, they are also deprived of their own public authority as rebels. Honoratus and Urbanus said to the bishops: The highest provision of your sanctity has stuck together in the minds of each one, and I think that by the response of all those things which you have deigned to pursue will be strengthened. All the bishops said: I like it, I like it.

XLIV. No bishop presumes to be a foreign cleric.

Epigonius the bishop said: In many councils this has been established, and even now this must be confirmed by your prudence, most blessed brothers, that no bishop should usurp a foreign cleric except at the discretion of him whose cleric he was. But I say that Julian, who was ungrateful for the favors of God conferred upon him by my littleness, was so rash and daring, that he who was baptized by me, when he was a child, was recommended to me by the same, and was nourished and raised by me for many years, as I have said. baptized in my church by the hand of my poverty, the same had begun to be a lector in the Appalian diocese, nay, he had read for nearly two years, I don't know with what contempt for my humility the same was seized by Julian, whom he says was unconscionably usurping me as a proper citizen of his local Baptistery; for he also ordained him a deacon: let this be clear, this license to us, most blessed brethren, if less he should be restrained so imprudently, that he should not mingle with the communion of any one. Bishop Numidius said. If Julian seems to have done this, neither at your request nor at your own condescension, we all judge the act unjustly or unworthily; therefore, unless the same Julian corrects his error, and with satisfaction recalls the same cleric whom he had dared to order to your people, acting contrary to the statutes of the council, he is separated from us for his insolence. he will receive judgment. Bishop Epigonius said: Father in age, the oldest in promotion, a praiseworthy man, our brother and colleague Victor, wants this general request to be made to all.

XLV. That a bishop who has several clerics should be given to those who need him for ordination.

Bishop Aurelius said: Accept my sermon, brothers: it sometimes happens that they are requested from churches that need presbyters or bishops, and yet, mindful of the statutes, I follow it, to meet with its bishop and impress upon him that its cleric is required by every church: but perhaps in the present day they have not relented, and lest it should ever happen that they relent, when they have been requested by me in this matter, whom you know to support the care of many churches and ordinations; devoutly has arisen, what does your charity consider to be done? For I bear the concern of all the churches, by the grace of God, as you know, brethren. Bishop Numidius said: This has always been the license of this see, to ordain a bishop from wherever he wished and in whose name the meeting was held, according to the desire of any one of the Church. Bishop Epigonius said: Goodness seizes the possibility, for you presume less, brother, when you render yourself good and merciful; for you have this at your discretion: it is sufficient to satisfy the persons of each bishop in the first agreement only; But if, even though I have sat here, he has thought to be vindicated, it is necessary for you to support all the churches: wherefore we do not give you power, but assign it to you, that it may be permitted to your will, and that you may always retain whom you will, that you may appoint superiors to the people or to the churches who have been requested. And where do you want it? Bishop Postumianus said: Then, who has one, must one priest himself be taken away from him? Bishop Aurelius said: But there can be one bishop, through whom many priests can be appointed by the divine condescension; but it is difficult to establish one bishop: therefore, if a necessary bishop has a priest, and if he has one, as you said, a brother, he will also have to give him for promotion. Bishop Postumianus said: Therefore, if another has abundant clerics, must another people help me? Bishop Aurelius said: Of course, how you help the other Church, he who has several clerics will be persuaded to give you one to ordain.

XLVI. That a bishop, having become a bishop in a diocese, should hold only the people in which he was ordained.

The bishops Honoratus and Urbanus said: We have heard it established that dioceses are not entitled to receive bishops, except with the consent of the one under whom they were established. but in our province, when some people in a diocese conceded to the bishop in whose power they had been appointed, the bishops were ordered to claim the dioceses for themselves: this must also be corrected by the judgment of your charity, and the rest must be checked. Epigonius, the bishop, said: It was reserved for each bishop what was proper, that no diocese should be chosen from the mass of dioceses to have its own bishop, unless he himself had used the consent to grant it. For it is sufficient if he consents, that the same diocese may have his own bishop only, and he will not claim for himself the other dioceses, which, apart from the band of many, alone deserved to receive the honor of the episcopate. Bishop Aurelius said: I have no doubt that your charity will please everyone in the diocese, by granting the bishop who held the matrix to retain only the people in which he was ordained.

XLVII. So that apart from the canonical Scriptures, nothing is read in the church under the name of the divine Scriptures.

Now there are canonical Scriptures, that is: 1. Genesis. 2. Exodus. 3. Leviticus. 4. Numbers. 5. Deuteronomy. 6. Jesus' Ship. 7. Judges. 8. Ruth. 9. Book IV of the Kingdoms. 10. Chronicles book 2 11. Job. 12. The Davidic Psalter. 13. The books of Solomon V. 14. The books of the 12 prophets. 15. Isaiah 16. Jeremiah 17. Ezekiel. 18. Daniel. 19. Tobias. 20. Judith. 21. Esther. 22. Book of Ezra II. 23. Book II of the Maccabees. And the New Testament. 24. Book IV of the Gospels 25. Book of the Acts of the Apostles I. 26. Epistles of Paul the Apostle XIII; the same to Hebrews 1. 27. Peter 2; John III; Jude 1; James I; Book 1 of the Apocalypse of John. Twenty-seven books are then made, in such a way that the overseas churches are consulted about confirming this canon. It is also permissible to read the passions of the martyrs, when their anniversaries are celebrated.

XLVIII. Of those baptized by the Donatists.

It was decided of the Donatists that we consult our brothers and fellow priests Siricius and Simplicianus about the only infants who are baptized near them, lest what they did not do by their own judgment, when they were converted to the Church of God with a wholesome purpose, the error of their parents should prevent them from being promoted as ministers of the holy altar. When they were joined, Honoratus and Urbanus, the bishops, ambassadors of the province of Mauritania, Sitiphensi, said: It has been a long time since we have been alleging the writings before your holiness, and we have been delayed by the contemplation that our brothers might arrive as ambassadors from Numidia. but because there are no small days in which they did not come at all when expected; It is not necessary to pass over what has been commanded us by our fellow-bishops; and therefore, brethren, gladly accept our suggestion. For we have heard the treatise of the Nicene faith, and the truth also concerning the prohibition of sacrifices after the meal, that they should be offered by fasting, as has been said, and it was confirmed then and now.

XLIX. Of those who have nothing and are ordained in the churches.

It was agreed that bishops, priests, deacons, or any clerics who have nothing and are ordained, and during their episcopate or clerical tenure acquire fields or any estates in their own name, as if they were held guilty of the crime of invasion of property, unless they were warned and contributed the same to the Church. But if something properly comes to them through the generosity of someone or through the succession of relatives, let them do what suits their purpose. that if they turn back from their intention, unworthy of ecclesiastical honor, they will be judged as reprobates.

L. That the deeds of the council of bishops be confirmed by their signatures.

Bishop Aurelius said: Since I think that all things have been dealt with, if all things agree with your mind, strengthen all things with your speech. All the bishops said: We have all been pleased with these things, and we will confirm them with our signature, and they signed them.

Aurelius, bishop of the Church of Carthage, consented to this decree, and read it and signed it.

Epigonius, bishop of the people of the region of Bull, subscribed.

Augustine, bishop of the people of Hippo, subscribed.

Likewise, all the forty-four bishops signed.

LATIN TEXT

CONCILIUM CARTHAGINENSE TERTIUM

HABITUM AB EPISCOPIS NUMERO QUADRAGINTA SEPTEM, AERA CCCCXXXVI, CAESARIO ET ATTICO VIRIS CLARISSIMIS CONSULIBUS

V KALENDAS SEPTEMBRIS.

Carthagine in secretario basilicae restitutae cum Aurelius episcopus una cum coepiscopis suis consedisset, astantibus etiam diaconibus, constituta sunt haec quae in praesenti concilio definita sunt.

I. Ut provinciales episcopi de pascha suum primatem inquirant. Placuit igitur in principio, propter errorem qui saepe solet oboriri, ut omnes Africanae provinciae episcopi observationem diei paschalis ab Ecclesia Carthaginensi curent accipere.

II. Ut per singulos annos concilium fiat.

Similiter placuit ut propter causas ecclesiasticas, quae ad perniciem plebium saepe veterascunt, singulis quibusque annis concilium convocetur, ad quod omnes provinciae quae primas sedes habent, de conciliis suis binos aut quantos elegerint episcopos legatos mittant; ut et minus invidiosi minusque hospitibus sumptuosi existant, et in congregato conventu plena possit esse auctoritas: de Tripoli autem propter inopiam episcoporum unus episcopus veniat.

III. Ut episcopus priusquam ordinetur canones agnoscat. Item placuit, ut ordinandis episcopis vel clericis prius ab ordinatoribus suis decreta conciliorum auribus eorum inculcentur, ne se aliquid contra statuta concilii fecisse poeniteant.

IV. Ut levitae et virgines ante viginti quinque annos non consecrentur. Item placuit, ut ante viginti quinque annos aetatis nec diacones ordinentur, nec virgines consecrentur, et ut lectores populum non salutent.

V. Ut sacramentum catechumenis non praebeatur.

Item placuit, ut etiam per solemnissimos paschales dies sacramentum catechumenis non detur, nisi solitum salis; quia si fideles per illos dies sacramenta non mutant, nec catechumenos oportet mutare.

VI. Ut mortuis baptismus vel eucharistia non detur.

Item placuit, ut corporibus defunctorum eucharistia non detur; dictum est enim a Domino: Accipite et edite: cadavera autem nec accipere possunt nec edere. Deinde cavendum est ne mortuos etiam baptizari posse fratrum infirmitas credat, quibus nec eucharistiam dari animadverterit.

VII. Ut si episcopus accusatur, ubi vel infra quod tempus examinetur.

Aurelius episcopus dixit: Quisquis episcoporum accusatur, ad primates provinciae ipsius causam deferat accusator, nec a communione suspendatur cui crimen intenditur, nisi ad causam suam dicendam primae sedis litteris evocatus die statuta minime occurrerit, hoc est intra spatium mensis ex ea die qua eum litteras accepisse constiterit: quod si aliquas veras necessitatis causas probaverit, quibus eum occurrere non potuisse manifestum sit, causae suae dicendae intra alterum mensem integram habeat facultatem; verumtamen diu post mensem secundum non communicet donec purgetur. Si autem nec ad concilium universale anniversarium occurrere voluerit ut vel ibi causa ejus terminetur, ipse in se damnationis sententiam dixisse judicetur; tempore sane quo non communicat, nec in sua ecclesia vel parochia communicet: accusator autem ejus si nunquam diebus causae dicendae defuerit a communione non removeatur; si vero aliquando defuerit subtrahens se, restituto in communionem episcopo, ipse removeatur a communione accusator, ita tamen ut nec ipsi adimatur facultas causae peragendae, si se ad diem occurrere non noluisse, sed non potuisse probaverit. Illud vero placuit, ut cum agere coeperit in episcoporum judicio, si fuerit accusatoris persona culpabilis, ad arguendum non admittatur, nisi proprias causas non tamen si ecclesiasticas asserere voluerit.

VIII. De presbyteris et diaconibus, quanti episcopi eos audiant.

Si autem presbyteri vel diaconi fuerint accusati, adjuncto sibi ex vicinis locis proprius episcopus legitimo numero collegarum, una secum in presbyteri nomine episcopi sex, in diaconi tres, ipsorum causam discutiant, eadem dierum et dilatione et a communione remotionum et discussione personarum inter accusatores et eos qui accusantur forma servata. Reliquorum autem clericorum causas etiam solus episcopus loci agnoscat et finiat.

IX. Ut clerici publica judicia non appellent.

Item placuit, ut quisquis episcoporum, presbyterorum et diaconorum seu clericorum, cum in Ecclesia ei fuerit crimen institutum vel civilis causa fuerit commota, si relicto judicio ecclesiastico publicis judiciis purgari voluerit, etiam si pro ipso fuerit prolata sententia, locum suum amittat; et hoc in criminali actione: in civili vero perdat quod evicit, si locum suum obtinere maluerit. Cui enim ad eligendos judices undique Ecclesiae patet auctoritas, ipse se indignum Ecclesiae consortio judicat, qui de universa Ecclesia male sentiendo de judicio saeculari poscit auxilium, cum privatorum Christianorum causas Apostolus etiam ad Ecclesiam deferri atque ibi determinari praecipiat.

X. Si quisque ab aliis judicibus ecclesiasticis ad alios fuerit, non obesse prioribus si diversa sententia proferatur. Hoc etiam placuit, ut a quibuscunque judicibus ecclesiasticis ad alios judices ecclesiasticos ubi est major auctoritas fuerit provocatum, non eis obsit quorum fuerit soluta sententia, si convinci non potuerint vel inimico animo judicasse vel aliqua cupiditate aut gratia depravati: sane si ex consensu partium judices electi fuerint, etiam a pauciori numero quam constitutum est non liceat provocari.

XI. Ut filii clericorum ad spectacula non accedant.

Ut filii sacerdotum vel clericorum spectacula saecularia non exhibeant, sed nec spectent, quandoquidem ab spectando etiam omnes laici prohibeantur; semper enim Christianis omnibus hoc interdictum est, ut ubi blasphemiae sunt non accedant.

XII. Ut filii clericorum matrimoniis infidelium non socientur.

Item placuit, ut filii vel filiae episcoporum vel quorumlibet clericorum Gentilibus vel haereticis aut schismaticis matrimonio non conjungantur.

XIII. Ut clerici de rebus suis nihil infidelibus conferant. Ut episcopi vel clerici in eos qui catholici Christiani non sunt, etiam si consanguinei fuerint, per donationes rerum suarum nihil conferant.

XIV. Ut clerici filios suos a sua potestate exire non sinant, nisi aetate et moribus comprobatis. Ut episcopi vel clerici filios suos a sua potestate per mancipationem exire non sinant, nisi de moriribus eorum fuerint et de aetate securi, ut possint ad eos jam propria pertinere peccata.

XV. Ut clerici non sint conductores vel negotiatores. Item placuit, ut episcopi, presbyteri et diaconi vel clerici non sint conductores aut procuratores privatorum, neque ullo turpi vel inhonesto negotio victum quaerant, quia respicere debent scriptum esse: Nemo militans Deo implicat se negotiis saecularibus.

XVI. Ut nullus clericus sit usurarius. Ut nullus clericorum amplius recipiat, quam cuiquam quod accommodaverit: si pecuniam, pecuniam accipiat: si speciem, speciem: quantum dederit accipiat: et quidquid aliud, tantum quantum dederit.

XVII. Ut cum clericis extraneae feminae non cohabitent.

Ut cum omnibus omnino clericis extraneae feminae non cohabitent, sed solae matres, aviae et materterae, amitae, sorores et filiae fratrum aut sororum, et quaecunque ex familia domestica necessitate, etiam antequam ordinarentur, jam cum eis habitabant, vel si filii eorum jam ordinatis parentibus uxores acceperunt, aut servis non habentibus in domo quas ducant, aliunde ducere necessitas fuerit.

XVIII. Ut clerici non ordinentur nisi omnes qui cum eis sunt fideles existant.

Ut episcopi et presbyteri et diaconi non ordinentur priusquam omnes qui sunt in domo eorum Christianos catholicos fecerint.

XIX. Ut clerici cum ad pubertatem venerint aut conjugium aut castitatem profiteantur. Placuit ut lectores, cum ad annos pubertatis venerint, cogantur aut uxores ducere aut continentiam profiteri

XX. Ut plebes alienas alius episcopus non usurpet. Placuit ut a nullo episcopo usurpentur plebes alienae, nec aliquis episcoporum supergrediatur in dioecesim collegae sui.

XXI. Ut nullus episcopus alienum clericum audeat retinere vel ordinare. Ut clericum alienum, nisi concedente ejus episcopo, nemo audeat retinere vel promovere in ecclesia sibi credita: clericorum autem nomen etiam lectores et psalmistae et ostiarii retinent.

XXII. Ut nullus clericus ordinetur, nisi fuerit vitae probabilis.

Ut nullus ordinetur clericus, nisi probatus vel episcoporum examine vel populi testimonio.

XXIII. De precibus et orationibus.

Ut nemo in precibus vel Patrem pro Filio, vel Filium pro Patre nominet; et cum altari assistitur semper ad Patrem dirigatur oratio; et quicunque sibi preces aliunde describit, non eis utatur, nisi prius eas cum instructionibus fratribus contulerit.

131 XXIV. Ut in sacrificio panis et calix offeratur. Ut in sacramentis corporis et sanguinis Domini nihil amplius offeratur quam ipse Dominus tradidit, hoc est panis et vinum aquae mistum, nec amplius in primitiis offeratur, quam de uvis et frumentis.

XXV. Ne clerici vel continentes ad virgines vel viduas soli habeant accessum. Ut clerici vel continentes ad viduas vel virgines nisi ex jussu vel permissu episcoporum aut presbyterorum non accedant, et hoc non soli faciant, sed cum conclericis vel cum his cum quibus episcopus aut presbyter jusserit; nec ipsi episcopi aut presbyteri soli habeant accessum ad hujusmodi feminas, sed ubi aut clerici praesentes sunt aut graves aliqui Christiani.

XXVI. Ut primae sedis episcopus princeps sacerdotum non appelletur. Ut primae sedis episcopus non appelletur princeps sacerdotum aut summus sacerdos aut aliquid hujusmodi, sed tantum primae sedis episcopus.

XXVII. Ut clerici tabernas non ingrediantur.

Ut clerici edendi vel bibendi causa tabernas non ingrediantur, nisi peregrinationis necessitate.

XXVIII. Ut episcopus sine formata metropolitani longius non proficiscatur.

Ut episcopi trans mare non proficiscantur, nisi consulto primae sedis episcopo suae cujusque provinciae, ut ab eo praecipue possit sumere formatam vel commendationem.

XXIX. Ut missa a jejuris celebretur. Ut sacramenta altaris non nisi a jejunis hominibus celebrentur; nam si aliquorum pomeridiano tempore defunctorum, sive episcoporum sive caeterorum, commendatio facienda est, solis orationibus fiat, si illi qui faciunt jam pransi inveniuntur.

XXX. Ut nullus in ecclesia convivetur. Ut nulli episcopi vel clerici in ecclesia conviventur, nisi forte transeuntes hospitiorum necessitate illic reficiant: populi etiam ab hujusmodi conviviis quantum fieri potest prohibeantur.

XXXI. Ut poenitentibus juxta peccatum modus poenitentiae detur. Ut poenitentibus secundum differentiam peccatorum episcopi arbitrio poenitentiae tempora decernantur.

XXXII. Ut presbyter praeter jussum vel absentiam episcopi non reconciliet poenitentem.

Ut presbyter inconsulto episcopo non reconciliet poenitentem, nisi absentia episcopi necessitate cogente: cujuscunque autem poenitentis publicum et vulgatissimum crimen est, quod universam Ecclesiam commoverit; ante absidam manus ei imponatur.

XXXIII. De custodia sacrarum virginum.

Ut virgines sacrae, si a parentibus a quibus custodiebantur privatae fuerint, episcopi providentia vel presbyteri ubi episcopus absens est, monasterio virginum vel gravioribus feminis commendentur, ut simul habitantes invicem se custodiant, ne passim vagando Ecclesiae laedant opinionem.

XXXIV. De baptizandis aegrotis qui jam loqui non possunt. Ut aegrotantes si pro se respondere non possunt, cum voluntatis eorum testimonium sui dixerint, baptizentur.

XXXV. Ut apostaticis et scenicis conversis reconciliatio non negetur. Ut scenicis atque histrionibus caeterisque hujusmodi personis, vel apostaticis conversis vel reversis ad Deum gratia vel reconciliatio non negetur.

XXXVI. Ut presbyter chrisma non conficiat.

Ut presbyter non consulto episcopo virgines non consecret; chrisma vero nunquam conficiat.

XXXVII. Ut clerici sine necessitate in aliena civitate non immorentur.

Ut clerici in aliena civitate non immorentur, nisi causas eorum justas episcopus loci vel presbyteres locorum perviderint.

XXXVIII. Ut non liceat fieri translationes episcoporum.

Illud autem suggerimus mandatum nobis, quod etiam in Capuensi plenaria synodo videtur statutum, ut non liceat fieri rebaptizationes, reordinationes vel translationes episcoporum: nam Crisconius Villaregiensis episcopus, plebe sua derelicta, Tubuniensem invasit ecclesiam, cujusque in hodie commonitus secundum quod statutum fuerat, relinquere eamdem quam invaserat plebem contempsit. Adversus istum quae pronuntiata fuerant confirmata quidem audivimus; sed petimus, secundum quod nobis mandatum est, ut dignemini dare fiduciam: quoniam necessitate ipsa cogente, liberum nobis sit rectorem provinciae secundum statuta gloriosissimorum principum adversus illum adire, ut qui miti admonitioni sanctitatis vetrae acquiescere noluit et emendare illicitum, auctoritate judiciaria protinus excludatur. Aurelius episcopus dixit: Servata forma disciplinae non aestimabitur appetitus si a vestra charitate modeste conventus recedere detrectaverit, cum fuerit suo contemptu et contumacia, faciente etiam auctoritate judiciaria, conventus. Honoratus et Urbanus episcopi dixerunt: Hoc ergo omnibus placet? Ab universis episcopis dictum est: Justum est, placet.

XXXIX. Ut non praesumant duo episcopi ordinare pontificem.

Honoratus et Urbanus episcopi dixerunt: Et illud nobis mandatum est, ut quia proxime fratres nostri Numidiae duo episcopi ordinare praesumpserunt pontificem, non nisi a duodecim censeatis episcoporum celebrari ordinationes. Aurelius episcopus dixit: Forma antiqua servabitur, ut non minus quam tres sufficiant, qui fuerint a metropolitano ordinati, ad episcopum ordinandum; propterea quia in Tripoli forte et in Arzuge interjacere videantur barbarae gentes; nam et in Tripoli, ut asseritur, episcopi sunt quinque tantum et possunt de ipso numero forte vel duo necessitate aliqua occupari, difficile est enim ut de quolibet numero omnes possint occurrere: nunquid debet hoc ipsum impedimento esse ecclesiasticae utilitati? Nam et in hac Ecclesia, ad quam dignata est sanctitas vestra convenire, crebro ac pene per diem dominicam ordinandos habemus: nunquidnam frequenter potero duodecim vel decem vel non multo minus advocare episcopos? sed facile est mihi duos adjungere meae parvitati vicinos: quapropter cernit mecum charitas vestra hoc ipsum observari non posse.

XL. Ut dum episcopus eligitur si contradictores habeat, quinque sacerdotes conveniant.

Et illud est statuendum, ut quando ad eligendum episcopum convenerimus, si qua contradictio fuerit oborta, quia talia facta sunt apud nos, non praesumant ad purgandum eum qui ordinandus est tres jam, sed postulentur ad numerum supradictorum duo vel tres, et in eadem plebe cui ordinandus est discutiantur primo personae contradicentium, postremo illa etiam quae objiciuntur pertractentur; et cum purgatus fuerit sub conspectu publico, ita demum ordinetur. Si hoc cum vestrae sanctitatis animo concordat, roboretur vestrae dignationis responsione. Ab universis episcopis dictum est: Satis placet.

XLI. Ut per singulos annos convenientes episcopi ad concilium etiam de paschali solemnitate a primate suo informentur.

Honoratus et Urbanus episcopi dixerunt: Quoniam de concilio quaedam tractata noscuntur, addimus etiam de die paschae nobis esse mandatum, ut de Ecclesia semper Carthaginensi, sicut praedictum est, instruamur et non sub angusto temporis spatio. Aurelius episcopus dixit: Si sanctitati vestrae videtur, quoniam nos spopondisse jam superius meminimus ut singulis quibusque annis ad tractandum conveniamus, et cum convenerimus in unum, tunc divulgabitur sanctus paschae dies per legatos qui adfuerint concilio. Honoratus et Urbanus episcopi dixerunt: Nunc de praesenti coetu petimus ut litteris provinciam nostram de hac die informare dignemini. Aurelius episcopus dixit: Ita fiat necesse est.

XLII. Ut non accipiat alium episcopum plebs quae in dioecesim semper subjacuit. Epigonius episcopus dixit: Multis conciliis hoc statutum est a coetu sacerdotali, ut plebes quae in dioecesibus ab episcopis retinentur, quae episcopos nunquam habuerunt, non nisi cum voluntate ejus episcopi a quo tenentur proprios accipiant rectores, id est episcopos: at vero quia nonnulli, dominatu quodam adepto, communionem fratrum abhorrent, vel certe cum depravati fuerint, quasi in quadam arce tyrannica sibi dominatum vindicant, quod plerique tumidi atque stolidi adversus episcopos suos cervices erigunt presbyteri, vel conviviis sibi conciliantes plebem vel certe persuasu maligno, ut illicito favore eosdem velint sibi collocare rectores, quod quidem insigne mentis tuae tenemus votum, frater religiose Aureli, quia haec saepe oppressisti non curando tales petitores, sed propter eorum malos cogitatus et prave concinnata concilia hoc dico: Non debere rectorem accipere eam plebem quae in dioecesim semper subjacuit, nec unquam proprium episcopum habuit; quapropter si universo sanctissimo coetui placet, hoc quod prosecutus sum confirmetur. Aurelius episcopus dixit: Fratres et consacerdotes nostri, prosecutioni non obsisto, sed hoc me et fecisse et facturum esse profiteor.

XLIII. Ut qui, plebe sua contempta, ad concilium venire detrectant et plebem et honorem amittant.

Circa eos sane qui fuerint concordes non solum circa Ecclesiam Carthaginensem, sed circa omne sacerdotale consortium, sunt enim plerique conspirantes cum plebibus propriis quas decipiunt, ut dictum est, earum scalpentes aures, blandi ad seducendum, vitiosae vitae homines, vel certe inflati et ab hoc consortio separati, qui putant propriae plebi incubandum et nonnunquam conventi ad concilium venire detrectant, sua forte ne prodantur flagitia metuentes; dico si placet circa hoc non tantum dioeceses non esse servandas, verum etiam et de propria Ecclesia, quae illis male faverit, omnimodo adnitendum ut etiam auctoritate publica rejiciantur, atque ab ipsis principalibus cathedris removeantur: oportet enim ut qui universis fratribus ac toto concilio inhaeserit, non solum suam jure integro, sed et dioeceses possideat; at vero qui sibimet putant plebes suas sufficere, fraterna dilectione contempta, non tantum dioeceses amittant, sed, ut dixi, etiam propriis publica careant auctoritate ut rebelles. Honoratus et Urbanus episcopi dixerunt: Summa provisio sanctitatis tuae cohaesit mentibus singulorum, et puto omnium responsione ea quae prosequi dignatus es roboranda. Universi episcopi dixerunt: Placet, placet.

XLIV. Ut clericum alienum nullus sibi praesumat episcopus.

Epigonius episcopus dixit: In multis conciliis hoc statutum est, etiam nunc hoc confirmandum a vestra prudentia, fratres beatissimi, ut clericum alienum nullus sibi praeripiat episcopus praeter ejus arbitrium cujus fuerit clericus. Dico autem Julianum, qui ingratus est Dei beneficiis per meam parvitatem in se collatis, ita temerarium et audacem exstitisse, ut eum qui a me baptizatus est, cum esset puer mihi ab eodem commendatus, cumque multis annis a me aleretur atque incresceret, hunc ut dixi baptizatum in Ecclesia mea per manum paupertatis meae, idem in dioecesi Appaliensi lector esse coeperat, imo annis ferme duobus legerat, nescio quo contemptu humilitatis meae idem Julianus arripuit, quem dicat quasi proprium civem sui loci Babtizaritani me inconsulto usurpare; nam et diaconum illum ordinavit: hoc scilicet pateat, haec licentia nobis, beatissimi fratres, si minus tam imprudens cohibeatur, ne se misceat communioni cujusquam. Numidius episcopus dixit: Si non postulata neque consulta tua dignatione id videtur fecisse Julianus, judicamus omnes inique factum vel indigne: quapropter nisi idem Julianus correxerit errorem suum, et cum satisfactione eumdem clericum quem fuerat ausus ordinare revocaverit tuae plebi, contra statuta concilii faciens, contumaciae suae separatus a nobis excipiet judicium. Epigonius episcopus dixit: Aetate pater, ipsa promotione antiquissimus, vir laudabilis, frater et collega noster Victor, vult hanc petitionem generalem omnibus effici.

XLV. Ut episcŏpus qui plures habet clericos ei qui eget ad ordinandum postulatus largiatur.

Aurelius episcopus dixit: Sermonem meum, admittite, fratres: contingit nonnunquam ut postulentur ab ecclesiis quae praepositis egent vel presbyteris vel episcopis, et tamen memor statutorum id sequor, ut conveniam episcopum ejus atque ei inculcem, quod ejus clericus a qualibet ecclesia postuletur: sed forte in hodierno non reluctati sunt, et ne quando contingat ut reluctentur, cum fuerint a me in hac causa postulati, quem scitis multarum ecclesiarum et ordinandorum curam sustinere, justum est ergo, ut quemlibet consacerdotum conveniam cum duobus e consortio nostro vel tribus testibus: si vero indevotus exstiterit, quid censet charitas vestra faciendum? ego enim cunctarum ecclesiarum dignatione Dei, ut scitis fratres, sollicitudinem sustineo. Numidius episcopus dixit: Fuit haec semper licentia huic sedi, ut unde vellet et de cujus nomine fuisset conventus, pro desiderio cujusquam Ecclesiae, ordinaret episcopum. Epigonius episcopus dixit: Bonitas sequestrat possibilitatem, minus enim praesumis, frater, cum te bonum et clementem reddis; habes enim hoc in arbitrio: satis est ut satisfaciat personae uniuscujusque episcopi in prima tantummodo conventione; si autem, quod licet huic sedi, vindicandum sibi fuerit arbitratus, necesse habes tu omnes ecclesias suffulcire: unde tibi non potestatem damus, sed tuae assignamus, ut liceat voluntati tuae et semper tenere quem voles, ut praepositos plebibus vel ecclesiis constituas qui fuerint postulati, et unde voles. Postumianus episcopus dixit: Deinde qui unum habuerit, nunquid debet illi unus ipse presbyter auferri? Aurelius episcopus dixit: Sed episcopus unus esse potest, per quem dignatione divina presbyteri multi constitui possint; unus autem episcopus difficile invenitur constituendus: quapropter si necessarium episcopus quis habuerit presbyterum, et unum, ut dixisti, frater, habuerit, etiam ipsum ad promotionem dare debebit. Postumianus episcopus dixit: Ergo si habet alius abundantes clericos, debet mihi alia plebs subvenire? Aurelius episcopus dixit:

Sane, quomodo tu Ecclesiae alteri subveneris, persuadebitur illi qui plures habet clericos, ut unum tibi ordinandum largiatur.

XLVI. Ut episcopus in dioecesi factus solam eam teneat plebem in qua exstitit ordinatus.

Honoratus et Urbanus episcopi dixerunt: Audivimus constitutum ut dioeceses non mereantur episcopos accipere, nisi consensu ejus sub quo fuerant constitutae; sed in provincia nostra, cum aliqui forte in dioecesi concedente eo episcopo in cujus potestate fuerant constitutae ordinati sunt episcopi, etiam dioeceses sibi vindicare: hoc et corrigi charitatis vestrae judicio et inhiberi debet de caetero. Epigonius episcopus dixit: Singulis episcopis servatum est quod decebat, ut ex massa dioecesium nulla carperetur ut proprium episcopum habuisset, nisi ipse consensum adhibuisset concedendi. Sufficiat enim si consenserit, ut eadem dioecesis permissa proprium tantum episcopum habeat, caeteras sibi non vindicet dioeceses, quae excepta de fasce multarum sola meruit honorem episcopatus suscipere. Aurelius episcopus dixit: Non dubito charitati vestrae omnium placere eum in dioecesi, concedente episcopo, qui matricem tenuit, solam eamdem retinere plebem in qua fuerit ordinatus.

XLVII. Ut praeter Scripturas canonicas nihil in ecclesia legatur sub nomine divinarum Scripturarum.

Sunt autem canonicae Scripturae, id est: 1. Genesis. 2. Exodus. 3. Leviticus. 4. Numeri. 5. Deuteronomium. 6. Jesu Nave. 7. Judicum. 8. Ruth. 9. Regnorum libri IV. 10. Paralipomenon libri II. 11. Job. 12. Psalterium Davidicum. 13. Salomonis libri V. 14. Libri XII prophetarum. 15. Esaias. 16. Jeremias. 17. Ezechiel. 18. Daniel. 19. Tobias. 20. Judith. 21. Esther. 22. Esdrae libri II. 23. Machabaeorum libri II. Novi autem Testamenti. 24. Evangeliorum libri IV. 25. Actuum apostolorum liber I. 26. Pauli apostoli Epistolae XIII; ejusdem ad Hebraeos I. 27. Petri II; Joannis III; Judae I; Jacobi I; Apocalypsis Joannis liber I. Fiunt igitur libri viginti et septem, ita ut de confirmando isto canone transmarinae Ecclesiae consulantur. Liceat etiam legi passiones martyrum, cum anniversarii dies eorum celebrantur.

XLVIII. De baptizatis a Donatistis.

De Donatistis placuit, ut consulamus fratres et consacerdotes nostros Siricium et Simplicianum de solis infantibus qui baptizantur penes eosdem, ne quod suo non fecerunt judicio, cum ad Ecclesiam Dei salubri proposito fuerint conversi, parentum illis error impediat ne promoveantur sacri altaris ministri. Quibus insertis, Honoratus et Urbanus episcopi legati provinciae Mauritaniae Sitiphensis dixerunt: Jam dudum cum apud sanctitatem vestram allegaremus scripta, dilati sumus ea contemplatione quod fratres nostri advenire possent de Numidia legati; sed quia non parvi dies sunt quibus exspectati minime venerunt; ultra praetermittere, quae nobis mandata sunt a nostris coepiscopis non oportet; atque ideo fratres suggestionem nostram libenter admittite. De fide enim Nicaeni tractatus audivimus, verum et de sacrificiis inhibendis post prandium, ut a jejunis sicut dictum est offerantur, et tunc et nunc firmatum est.

XLIX. De his qui nihil habentes in ecclesiis ordinantur.

Placuit ut episcopi, presbyteri, diaconi vel quicunque clerici, qui nihil habentes ordinantur, et tempore episcopatus vel clericatus sui agros vel quaecunque praedia nomini suo comparant, tanquam rerum dominicarum invasionis crimine teneantur, nisi admoniti in Ecclesiam eadem ipsa contulerint. Si autem ipsis proprie aliquid liberalitate alicujus vel successione cognationis venerit, faciant inde quod eorum proposito congruit; quod si a suo proposito retrorsum exorbitaverint honore ecclesiastico indigni, tanquam reprobi judicentur.

L. Ut gesta concilii episcoporum subscriptionibus confirmentur.

Aurelius episcopus dixit: Quoniam igitur universa arbitror fuisse tractata, si omnia cum animo vestro convenerint, sermone vestro cuncta roborate. Universi episcopi dixerunt: Omnibus nobis haec placuerunt, et haec nostra subscriptione firmabimus, Et subscripserunt.

Aurelius episcopus Ecclesiae Carthaginis huic decreto consensi, et relecto subscripsi.

Epigonius episcopus plebis Bullensis regionis subscripsi.

Augustinus episcopus plebis Hipponensium regionum subscripsi.

Similiter et omnes episcopi quadraginta quatuor subscripserunt.

The Scriptorium Project is the work of a small group of lay people of various apostolic churches who are interested in the preservation, transmission, and translation of the works of the early and medieval church. Our efforts are to make the works of the church fathers accessible to anyone who might have an interest in Christian antiquities and the theological, philosophical, and moral writings that have become the bedrock of Western Civilization.

To-date, our releases have pulled from the Greek, Syriac, Georgian, Latin, Celtic, Ethiopian, and Coptic traditions of Christianity, and have been pulled from sundry local traditions and languages.

Other Catalogue Titles for the Early Punic Church in North Africa:

Seven Rules by Ticonius the Donatist *(July 2006)*
Letters on the Council of Ephesus by Capreolus of Carthage (Aug. 2007)
The Time of the Barbarians by St. Quoddeusvult of Carthage (Feb. 2009)
3rd Council of Carthage by Gratus of Carthage (Oct. 2010)
4th Council of Carthage by Geneclius of Carthage (Nov. 2010)
5th Council of Carthage by St. Aurelius of Carthage (Dec. 2010)
Two Letters from Byzantine Africa by Licinianus of Carthage (Oct. 2016)
Apology to Gunthamund, King of Vandals by Blossius Aemilius Dracontius (Feb. 2018)
Letter to Pope Theodore by Victor of Carthage (Feb. 2020)
Council of Mileum by St. Aurelius of Carthage (Aug. 2022)
Council of Zella by Donatianus of Zella (Sept. 2022)
Against Palladius the Arian by Vigilius of Thapsus (Nov. 2023)
Response Against Arians by St. Fulgentius of Ruspe (Jan. 2024)
The Final Letter to Latin North Africa by Pope Leo IX (Mar. 2024)
Letters & Pamphlets by Fulgentius Ferrandus (Apr. 2024)

www.ingramcontent.com/pod-product-compliance
Lightning Source LLC
LaVergne TN
LVHW010416070526
838199LV00064B/5315